Chickadees

By Whitney Webb

Computer stuff by Grandpa Bob

Now give me some Sugar!!

ISBN: 9798518528055
Published by: Chickadee Publications

The childhood art I have saved from my children is ZERO! I found these items a few days before Whitney's graduation from the 6th grade so I thought, "Something to remember her childhood." The process I used was simple: Take a picture with my phone, copy it to a Kindle template (You'll have to look it up,) and publish it on Kindle Direct Printing AKA KDP.

The first section, "Chickadees" is from Whitney's, 5 X 4 booklet with ten pages. The second segment, "Playing on The Diamond" is copied from a 9 X 14 booklet. A little twisting and turning and the pages make a nice 8.5 X 11 booklet.

This is a great example of the potential for your collections. When you put them into an ebook, you have all your bases covered and a lifetime of memories. You can learn how to publish your books in that famous workbook, "It's Time to Write Your Memoir" which is written by my favorite author. You can pickup a copy on Amazon. Now enjoy Whitney's Genius!

Chickadees
By: Whitney Webb

Glossary

1. Wood Pecker- A bird that Pecks at wood.
2. Forst edge- where the trees meet the road.
3. interior- inside
4. desighn- the model such as a couch, kitchen, bedroom
5. black bib- this part
6. Chararistic- A person or things Perschality

Fact or Fib?

Chickadees nest in alive trees.

-alive tree

Fib!

Chickadees nest in dead trees and Sometimes old wood Peckers holes. Also they like bird houses and Pots. Chickadees start to nest around April and they stop laying eggs around June and lay up to 13 eggs.

Chickadees nest

Awesome job explaining your fib!

There are 13 eggs in Chickadees nest

Fact or Fib?
Chickadees live
near the forest edge.

Fact!
Chickadees live near the forest edge bcuasc there's normaly easier houses to spot. In forests theres mostly old trees with old wood pecker holes. And its like a mansion for chickadees!
What we see VS what Chickadees see
I did it!
Per-fect
fun fact both males and females work on the interior designer.
Love your voice here!!

Fact or Fib?

Chickadees love to eat nuts.

- wall nut

berries

ooo my fav!

Fib!

Chickadees do not eat nuts. Chickadees perfer berries, insects, small insectss. During breeding season the female "begs" for food then the male gets the food. While the female makes the nest and incubates the eggs.

FINE

Please get food

Great word choice!!

Fact or Fib?
You can tell the female and male Chickadees apart by the black bib.
why couldnt She get food

Fact!

You can tell chickadees apart by there black bib. Also by there characteristic the male is more domante. Next, the feamale is less donamate and isn't out getting food so you will most likly see more males than female in your back yard.

why did I agree

(4) Excellent! Thank you for working hard and making it interesting to read!

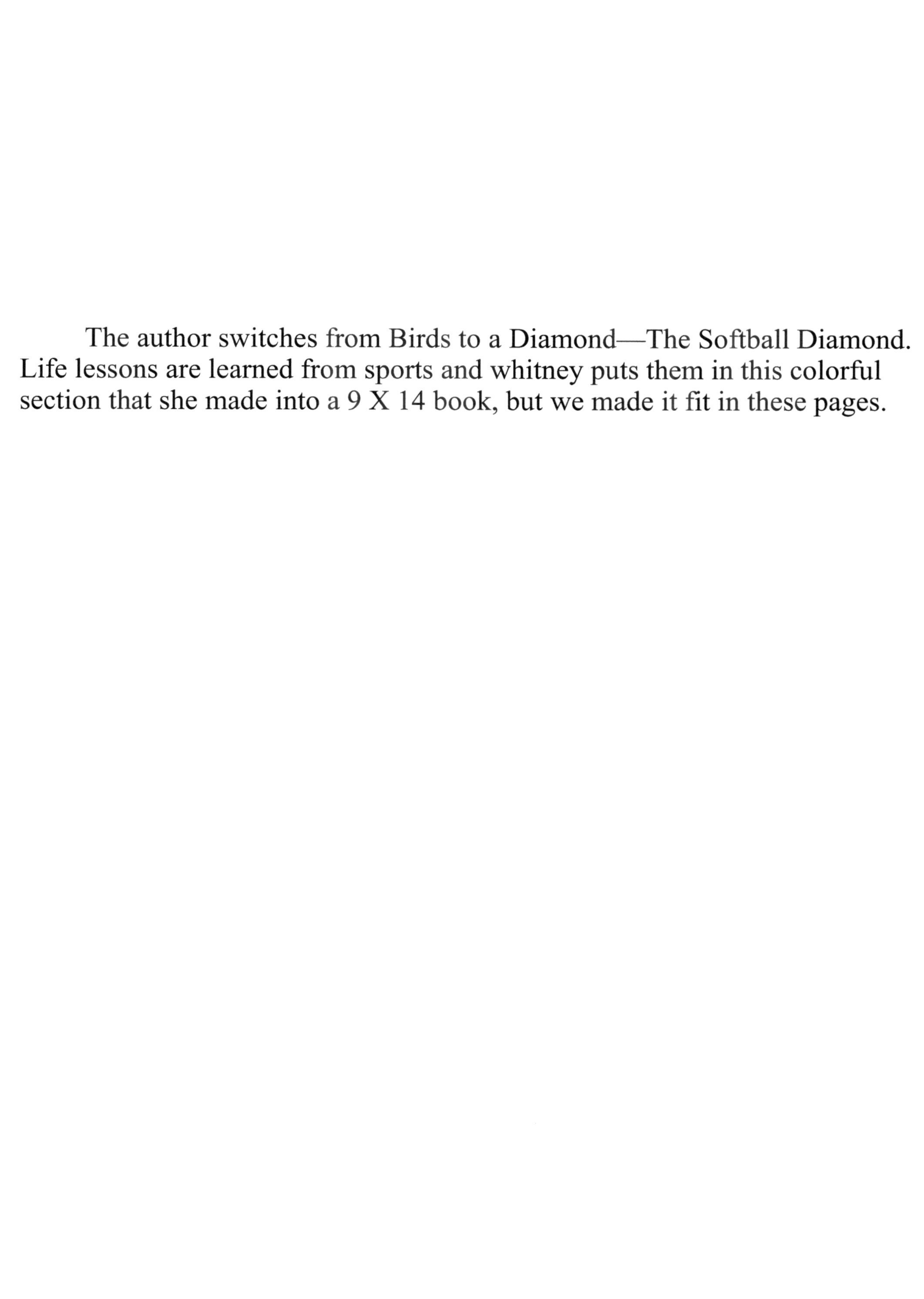

The author switches from Birds to a Diamond—The Softball Diamond. Life lessons are learned from sports and whitney puts them in this colorful section that she made into a 9 X 14 book, but we made it fit in these pages.

Playing On The Diamond

By: Whitney Webb

The Effect In Pitching With Weighted balls

Did you know that pitching with weighted balls has good and bad effects? A good effect is you are really powerful in your pitch. Second you learn to get the right form your supposed to. As a result you get a little messed up **release** point but not if you have the perfect warm up. That's why pitching with weighted balls effects you.

Gear You Need To Play

Gear in softball is really important and there's a lot of gear. For example a bat is really important in softball. I recommend metal bats they hit far and well. Normally bats come with grips which you need as well. Second, a glove is EXTREMELY important because you need it for feilding and I recommend a leather glove. My dad has had one since college that he it is still still intact. This next thing depends on the experience if you are scared of the ball, a chest guard is the best thing for you. Fourth, cleats are things that grip the ground and make you run a little faster as well you feel like a real softball player. This depends on you. If you're interested in being a catcher you need a ton of gear. For example, you need a helmet, shin guards,catcher's glove and a chest guard. I know my bat stung when I hit a good pitched ball until I got batting gloves. They help a ton now I can hit without them but they're good to still use. Now for pitching you might want a face mask because if a line drive is going straight for your head it wont give you a concussion. A helmet you have to have in order to bat you really should get because you are gonna hit. You see gear is not the most important thing in softball it's the skill.

Softball vs Baseball

If you think softball and baseball are the same then you should think again. Although they are very similar they are very different too. First let's talk about the ball size: a softball is bright yellow and big and a baseball is small and white. These too competitive sports have the same **fundamentals** for example pitchers,catchers,baters and much much more! Did you know baseball has a larger field then softball due to it being a lot easier to hit a light ball over a fence but a heavy big ball is a little more difficult. Next there pitching is a lot different as well. softball players pitch in a circle type motion but baseball players pitch in a throw type motion. Also baseball is more popular which means they get a little more money then softball because softball isaint as popular. These sports have a diamond shaped field. Lastly these astonishing sports both have Umpire that monitor strikes and balls or safe and out. These are the similarities and difference of softball and baseball.

How To Dive and slide

Diving and sliding in softball is a big part of softball. In order to not get out in softball you have to dive or slide. First run and lay back a little. Next, tuck your right leg behind the other. Lastly, put your hands to the ground and stand up but make sure your foot touches the bag. Now diving is a little different. First you run then put your hands up while diving towards the ground. Next head first touch the bag with your hands and stand up with a lim at least touching the bag. This why diving and sliding are really important.

A girl is diveing intoabase

A girl is slideing inta a base

Problem And Solution Of The Diamond

In softball it's all about staying strong inside the head and these are all issues and solutions about it. You know when you miss a ball over and over all you have to do is focus on the ball and follow it all the way through. When you just can't hit a ball far all you have to do is practice on a **tee.** When you swing low or high use a tee and swing slowly and hit the middle of the then u can start to swing faster. This is common during a live game you get stressed but all you have to think is " its okay to get out everyone does." You just have to try again. When you aren't able to hit the ball in a game not due to stress just step out and swing three times and get back in. lastly when your bats too heavy for you scoot your hands up on the grip or get a new bat. Even though there's a lot of problems in softball but a also lot of solutions.

GLOSSARY

Release-letting go of object

Tee-A thing like a base with a stick sticking out of the base and you put the ball on top

Fundamentals-small little things you need to master to be a good ball player

Great job, Whitney!
You have amazing ideas
and use transitions.
You could work on editing
for errors (capitalization, punctuation)

QUIZ TIME!!!!!!!!!

What is two effects from pitching with weighted balls?

1.It has no effects! Haha

2.It helps with making lemonade duh!

3.It helps with your power

4.It messes your realse up a little

What helps with swing to low?

1.swinging low over and over

2.hitting off a tee

3.you just hit the low pitches

4.you just practice on hitting more

What do catchers need to be a catcher?

1.All the gear in the world

2.helmet, chest guard, shin guards

3. Nothing they just play

4. Nailpolish duh!

The End

BUT LIKE THE CHICKADEES, WHITNEY'S JUST LEARNING TO FLY!!

www.ingramcontent.com/pod-product-compliance
Ingram Content Group UK Ltd.
Pitfield, Milton Keynes, MK11 3LW, UK
UKHW060122300726
14090UKWH00002B/320

* 9 7 9 8 5 1 8 5 2 8 0 5 5 *